Delete! Delete!

Written by Ian MacDonald
Illustrated by Alex Patrick

April and Pete like to play games. They never cheat and are brilliant gamers.

The screen freezes. Pete hits the DELETE button.
April lets out a shriek. "What's happening?"
"April!" Pete yells.

Pete spots April ... on the screen! She lets out a squeak as someone speaks.

"I am the Button Chief," it states.

You cannot leave until you reach level three. Collect a button on each level. If you fail, you will stay in this game.

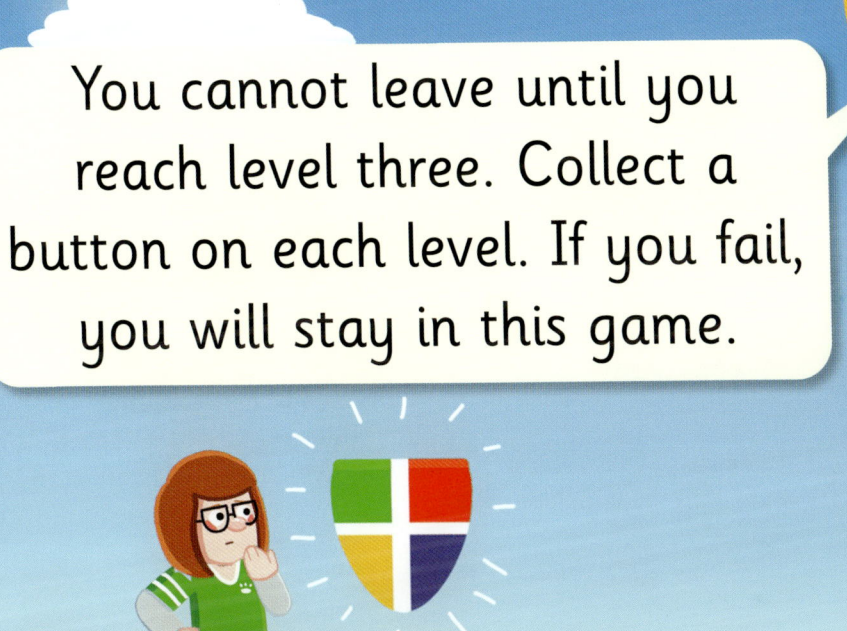

All of a sudden, a dragon appears next to April. A button is hanging from its neck!

LEVEL 1

"Grab that shield!" yells Pete.

A streak of flame hits April's shield as April leaps up to grab the button. The defeated dragon lands in a heap!

LEVEL 1

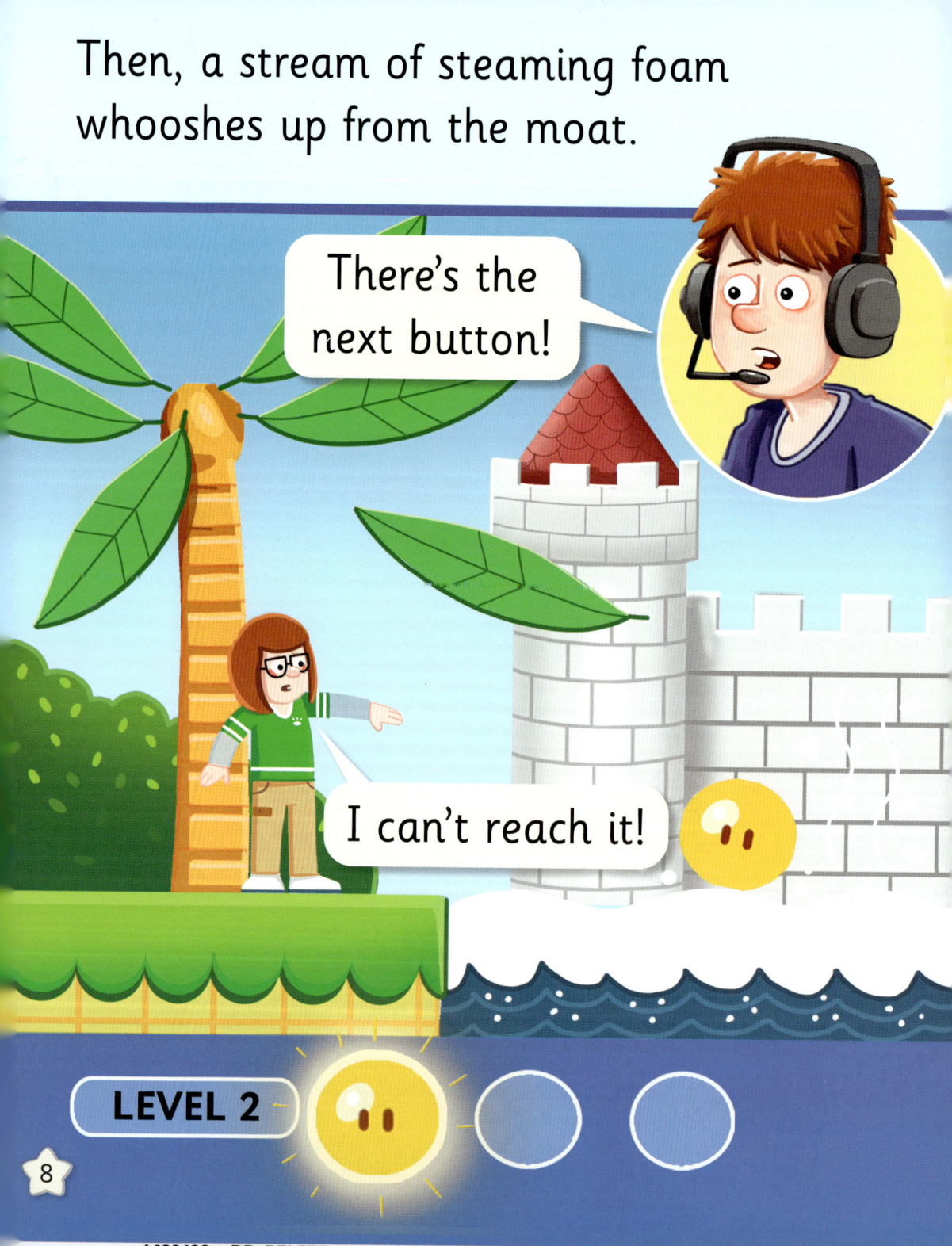

"Can you reach the button with this leaf?" asks Pete.
April leans across the stream and scoops up the button.

Pete eats an apricot cookie as he tracks April on the screen. The peaches are leading her to a field of peacocks.

April grabs the button as it drops from the mean peacock's beak.

Pete grins as April lands in her seat. Mum pops in. "As a treat, I've made extra cookies. They're peach ones!"

Talk about the story

Answer the questions:

1 Who told April the rules of the game?

2 Who did April defeat first?

3 What did April use to reach the second button?

4 How did the peaches help April?

5 How would you feel if you were inside the game?

6 What games do you like to play?

Can you retell the story in your own words?